TITUS SALT AND SALT

Industry and Virtue

by John Styles

The author, John Styles, was born and brought up in Bradford. He is currently Head of the M.A. Course in the History of Design at the Victoria and Albert Museum, London.

ISBN 0 9516950 0 2

Salts Estates Ltd., Victoria Road, Saltaire, Shipley, West Yorkshire, BD18 3LB, England.

All photographic work by Jonathan Silver except:
Bradford Industrial Museum (pages 10, 30, 32 & 34), Bolling Hall Museum, Bradford (page 15), Bradford Heritage Recording Unit (page 19), Pete Shaw of Baildon (page 17).

Designed by Ian Suffield at Art Direction (0274 531011).

The village of Saltaire, built by the industrialist Titus Salt between 1851 and 1872, lies tucked in the valley of the river Aire, three miles from the centre of the city of Bradford. Its situation is a surprisingly discreet one. Neither the vast mill complex in the valley bottom, six stories high and one hundred and eighty yards long, nor the twenty-five acre model village, laid out on a rectilinear plan across the southern slopes of the valley above the mill, entirely dominate the local landscape. Their Italianate architecture is striking, sometimes monumental, yet they do not command their surroundings in the manner of Samuel Cunliffe Lister's equally massive Manningham Mill, built in the 1870s, which rears up on the Bradford skyline from the rooftops of row upon row of terraced houses. At Saltaire the city seems far away. The overall impression is intimate as well as grand, pastoral as well as industrial.

This intimate, pastoral quality tells us much about Titus Salt's purpose in building his model industrial village. Although Saltaire was established in what was then open country divided by hills from the town of Bradford, its site and its character owed everything to Salt's experience of the town in the tumultuous decades of the 1830s and 1840s. Bradford's staple worsted industry grew at an explosive rate during these years. So did its population. Rapid growth brought many benefits, among the most prominent being cheaper clothing for consumers at home and overseas, and jobs for the town's new inhabitants. But growth took the form of a dizzy sequence of booms and slumps. It was accompanied by repeated bouts of mass unemployment, persistent technological unemployment among hand workers who were replaced by newly-invented machines, political conflict in the streets, industrial pollution, epidemics, drunkenness and filth.

Salt's new mill and village were to be everything Bradford was not. They were designed to nurture self-improvement, politeness, orderly behaviour, and good health among his workers. Salt's aim was to construct a successful company village, separate from the town, organised and ordered according to these objectives. In so doing, he intended to demonstrate that factories, the capitalist free market, and the amassing of great industrial fortunes like his own were compatible with material comfort and moral virtue among the working classes.

The audience he wished to persuade included both the industrial workers themselves and the many sceptics among the ranks of the well-educated and the socially privileged. That audience also embraced his fellow industrialists - his peers. They too were to be educated in virtue

The mill soon after completion.

by Saltaire. They were to be shown that great wealth carried great responsibilities; that it was the Christian duty of the virtuous employer to promote the material and moral well-being of his workpeople and his town.

By these means Salt achieved pre-eminence among his fellow Bradfordians. He was already active and respected in the life of Bradford before he built Saltaire. Once his moral and social ideas found physical expression in the mill, the terrace houses and the public buildings of his model village, he enjoyed yet more acclaim. Adulation came not only from his fellow Bradfordians, but from wealthy, educated and powerful men elsewhere in Britain and overseas; men who were terrified the explosive growth of the new factory industries would produce such moral degeneration and political subversion among the working classes that the established order would be toppled. Saltaire suggested it was possible to reconcile industrial expansion and social stability.

The village and the mill may not dominate the Bradford skyline like some of the town's other nineteenth-century civic and industrial buildings. Nevertheless Saltaire and the vision that gave it shape helped to make Titus Salt nationally and internationally famous, the greatest public figure of the Victorian era in Bradford, a legend.

Titus Salt: the man and his times.

Titus Salt is something of an enigma. He was one of Bradford's most prominent businessman and was extremely active in the life of the town. He served as Bradford's mayor and as its member of parliament. He enjoyed a reputation as a great local philanthropist, giving money to educational, religious and medical charities. Yet despite his prominence in civic affairs, Salt was a withdrawn, reticent, intensely private man. He found speaking in public excruciatingly difficult and was, by general agreement, bad at it. During his two years in the House of Commons he made not one speech in a debate. He was an unenthusiastic letter writer. Very little survives of either his private correspondence or the records of his business. As a consequence, his thoughts and plans remain difficult to decipher. We have, at Saltaire, the physical realisation of his ideas, and it can tell us much about the man, but the streets and buildings of his model village are not an open book from which we can read his intentions. If we are to reconstruct the beliefs and the hopes, the prejudices and the fears that informed his public life, we have to set what he did (and what little survives of what he said) against the wider canvas of life in Bradford in the first half of the nineteenth century.

In most accounts of the history of England between 1780 and 1850 it is the Industrial Revolution that holds centre stage. According to such accounts, a series of new inventions in textile manufacturing and steam motive power - Hargreaves' spinning jenny, Arkwright's water frame, Boulton and Watt's reciprocating steam engine - brought about a transformation in the English economy and in English society. Combined within the walls of the factory, these innovations, so the conventional account tells us, generated revolutionary changes. England ceased to be a predominantly agrarian, rural society. Instead it became industrial and urban.

This conventional narrative undoubtedly presents much too stark a contrast between the mid-eighteenth century and the mid-nineteenth century, as far as the history of England as a whole is concerned. By comparison with the industrialising nations of the twentieth century, countries like Japan and Korea, change in England during this period was slow and uneven. But if we focus our attention more narrowly and concentrate on those places, particularly in the Midlands and the north of England, where the new industries took root and flourished, then the conventional picture of dramatic upheaval is an accurate one. Bradford was such a place.

The warping room at Salts in the early twentieth century.

Twisting machinery at Salts in the early twentieth century.

At the beginning of the nineteenth century, in 1801, the population of what was later to become the borough of Bradford was barely thirteen thousand. Fifty years later, in 1851, the population had increased more than sevenfold to over one hundred thousand. In the course of half a century Bradford metamorphosed from a collection of small weaving villages into a major industrial town. Indeed Bradford was the fastest growing industrial town in England in this period. The motor of its spectacular increase in size was the manufacture of worsted cloth, which was the foundation of the town's prosperity.

Worsted cloth had been made in the Bradford area by hand techniques since the late-seventeenth century, but between 1800 and 1850 the productive capacity of the industry underwent a staggering increase. One-by-one the chief processes which converted raw wool into cloth were mechanised. The first process in which machines replaced hand production was the spinning of wool into yarn, at the beginning of the century. Later, from the 1820s, weaving yarn into cloth was gradually but inexorably taken over by power looms. Finally, from the late 1840s, machines were introduced to undertake the difficult task of combing the wool to prepare it for spinning. By 1851 there were 129 steam factories in the town. Before 1800 there had been none.

Mechanisation resulted in cheaper prices for cloth and a huge increase in the quantity produced. Worsted fabrics were manufactured in Bradford's new factories to a wide variety of standards and prices. Their final use was generally as clothes or furnishings. The single most important market for the Bradford industry appears to have been fabric for women's dresses. Women wore Bradford worsteds not only in England, but in the United States (a particularly important export market) and in many countries in continental Europe. Indeed by 1850 Bradford was more than just the capital of the British worsted industry; it had become its world centre.

In the process, the town attracted tens of thousands of migrants in search of work, mainly from Yorkshire and adjacent counties, but some from as far away as Ireland. Work in the worsted trade was hard and could be dangerous. The hours in the new factories, which employed mainly women and children, were long - before the Factory Act of 1833, sometimes twelve hours a day, six days a week, even for young children. Male hand loom weavers and hand woolcombers also worked long hours, often in polluted workshops. But the industry enjoyed many buoyant years during the first half of the nineteenth century. In such years, work, though arduous, was plentiful and relatively well paid.

Bradford from Undercliffe in 1873.

Men and women, especially young men and women, flocked to Bradford.

The town was ill-prepared to receive them and the families they raised. It was built quickly. As a result, it was often built badly. Yet the pace of building, fast as it was, failed to keep up with the demand for accommodation from the ever-expanding population. Roads, sewers and other public facilities were grossly inadequate. The consequences for many of the town's poorer inhabitants were overcrowding, pollution, and ill-health. Indeed by the 1840s the town was approaching an ecological crisis.

The two waterways that ran through the town - Bradford Beck and the Bradford canal - were open sewers, overloaded with domestic and industrial effluent. In the 1840s the canal was popularly known as "River Stink". The town was notorious for the smoke that poured from its ever-multiplying factory chimneys, irritating throats and lungs, and soiling clothes and buildings. Housing conditions for the poorest inhabitants were appalling. A survey in 1845 among hand woolcombers, one of the most impoverished trades, revealed cases of eight or twelve people living and working in just two rooms. Others inhabited dank, overcrowded cellars, which often flooded when it rained. Men and women slept three, four, or five to a bed.

Not all the town's working population had to endure such degraded housing, but it was the lot of thousands. Those fortunate enough to enjoy better accommodation still had to put up with impure water, rudimentary sewage disposal and atmospheric pollution. The result, in an age before antibiotics, was an extremely high death rate from infectious diseases, like smallpox and tuberculosis. Average expectation of life in the town in the 1840s was barely twenty years, the lowest in Yorkshire. The rate of infant mortality was the fifth highest in the country. A cholera epidemic killed 426 people in 1849.

Throughout Britain, the 1830s and 1840s were a period of social and political upheaval. Not surprisingly, Bradford was notorious as a centre of political agitation. The experience of privation and squalor generated enormous discontent among working people. So too did the wealth and power enjoyed by the men who owned Bradford's factories. To many workers, the immense fortunes accumulated by the local "millocrats" appeared to arise directly out of the conditions that made life in Bradford so unpleasant. Pollution and unemployment, it was argued, resulted from the "factory lords" pursuing their own profits without any thought for the rest of the town's population. Their mills poured soot into the skies and waste into the streams. They obliged their employees to work at the new machinery for extremely long hours, like slaves. They appeared to impoverish the hand workers by keeping the machines running so intensively. Many of the millowners, moreover, tried to block the enactment of new laws to control these abuses.

Popular discontent was expressed at meetings and rallies, demonstrations and riots. Bradford was a town where tens of thousands of people took to the streets to demand limits on hours of work in factories, official assistance for unemployed hand loom weavers and woolcombers, and the repeal of the hated New Poor Law. Above all, Bradfordians claimed the right to vote. Britain in the nineteenth century was not a democratic country. In 1840, less than one adult man in ten could vote, and no women. The power to vote was restricted to the very wealthy. Among the vast numbers of men and women denied the vote, many came to believe that repeated bouts of mass unemployment, long hours in the factories, and the threat of the workhouse for the destitute were the result of the undemocratic franchise. Governments elected by a tiny, privileged and self-interested minority were, they believed, directly responsible for the privations suffered by the majority. Democracy would sweep away a corrupt political system and promote the material well-being of the masses.

During the late 1830s and the 1840s the Chartist movement, which advocated votes for all adult males, was the principal vehicle for these political dissatisfactions. Bradford, with its discontented factory hands and its handloom weavers displaced by new technology, was notorious as a centre of Chartist agitation. Bradford's Chartists organised petitions and demonstrations. They also prepared weapons, drilled openly, and threatened to take over the town by force. So alarmed were the authorities that they stationed troops in Bradford. In 1842 and 1848 soldiers were deployed in the streets when the Chartists threatened to take over the town.

It was against this background of political violence, environmental degradation, and repeated mass unemployment that in the late 1840s Titus Salt conceived his plan to build his new factory and model village at Saltaire. Bradford in the 1840s had been a scene of turmoil; Saltaire was to nurture harmony. Many of Bradford's inhabitants believed the relationship of factory owner and factory hand resembled that of master and slave; Saltaire was to demonstrate the fellowship of the productive classes, embracing both employer and employed. Bradford was polluted, unhealthy and immoral; at Saltaire the physical, material and moral improvement of the workers was to

Titus Salt in 1856: a bust presented by his workers.

be promoted by a good employer. What were the means by which Salt aimed to achieve these goals?

Making cloth.

Even before he started to build Saltaire, Titus Salt enjoyed a formidable reputation as a model employer. In Bradford in the 1830s and 1840s many factory owners were regarded with hatred by large sections of the town's working population. Nevertheless, many working class political leaders were prepared to acknowledge that there were good as well as bad employers. Titus Salt was repeatedly identified as "one of the best masters in the town" and an example of how factory owners should behave.

Salt came to Bradford with his father from Crofton near Wakefield in 1822, when he was nineteen. At Crofton his father had been a farmer, comfortably off, but not rich. Titus, after working for several years in his father's new business supplying wool to Bradford manufacturers, set up his own worsted manufacturing firm in Bradford in 1834. By the mid-1840s he had made a fortune and had become one of the town's largest employers. He had five mills on different sites in the town and employed many hand loom weavers and hand combers in their own homes in Bradford and the surrounding villages. His reputation as a model employer was founded on his record of paying good wages and his reluctance to lay off his workforce, even during slumps.

Salt's beneficence towards his workforce was not simply the outcome of his own strongly-held religious and moral beliefs. It would have been impossible had his business not been such a spectacular success. Salt was able to treat his workers better than less successful manufacturers in the 1840s precisely because he was making a fortune. The key to the success of his business was its specialisation. Whereas the majority of firms in the Bradford worsted industry at this period made cloth from a combination of sheep's wool and cotton, Salt concentrated on fabrics made from alpaca (the hair of a South American llama) and mohair (the hair of the Angora goat), combined with cotton or silk. Alpaca and mohair were exotic, expensive raw materials, available only in small quantities. But alpaca, in particular, was extremely well suited to producing cloth with a brilliant, lustrous appearance that was very popular for women's dress fabrics during the middle decades of the nineteenth century.

Alpaca and mohair enabled Salt's firm to out-perform many other Bradford manufacturers.

Having already experimented with other exotic raw materials, he was one of the first businessmen in the town to make fabrics from alpaca and mohair successfully. In combination with a couple of other big manufacturers, he was able to buy up most of the available supplies of these scarce raw materials. He consequently enjoyed a semi-monopoly in a luxury market that was more resistant to trade depressions than other branches of the worsted industry.

The difficulty of obtaining regular supplies of alpaca and mohair from South America and Turkey provided the opportunity for Salt and two other manufacturers to operate as a secret cartel, buying up the available stocks as they arrived in England. By this means they excluded other manufacturers from the trade and assured themselves a lucrative monopoly. Alpaca and mohair were expensive and so were the fabrics made from them. They sold to wealthier customers whose purchases were resilient in the face of economic downswings. By concentrating on products made from these fashionable materials, Salt assured himself a buoyant, niche market. He avoided the worst of the violent downturns in demand which plagued the highly competitive mass market for the cheaper fabrics made from wool and cotton. Hence he escaped many of the losses suffered in hard times by those who manufactured the cheaper cloths.

Alpaca and mohair gave Titus Salt the resources to be a model employer and to build Saltaire. They also shaped the way his vast Saltaire factory was designed and the kind of work that went on there. The Saltaire mill was not a typical mid-nineteenth century Bradford factory. It was enormous in size, much bigger than other mills in the town. It was also an integrated works combining on a single site almost all the processes of manufacture. Bales of raw mohair and alpaca arrived at the factory on canal barges or railway trucks. Finished cloth left it by the same means, destined for customers all over Britain, Europe and North America.

Integration of this sort was unusual in the Bradford worsted industry. Salt himself, before his move to Saltaire in 1853, had at least five separate mills in Bradford for spinning and weaving, and put work out to hand loom weavers and hand woolcombers. This disaggregated pattern continued to be common in the Bradford worsted trade after 1850, when weaving and woolcombing were completely mechanized. Indeed, during the second half of the nineteenth century individual firms and their mills increasingly came to concentrate on single processes: on spinning, or on weaving, or

A fashion plate for 1862. The right-hand dress was to be made of cinnamon coloured alpaca and the child's dress of white alpaca.

on woolcombing. Integration made sense for Salt, however. In part, this was because he had the vast financial resources necessary to build a huge, integrated plant. It was also because the manufacture of his distinctive, high-quality products required special skills and careful supervision. These were most effectively provided on a single site.

The Saltaire factory was the marvel of its age. Built between 1851 and 1853, it was enormous, ultra-modern, and expensively ornate. Even today, in an era familiar with much bigger industrial units - steel mills, motor vehicle assembly plants and chemical works - its size continues to impress the visitor. It had six stories and a floor space of eleven and a half acres. More than three thousand people were employed when it was fully working and thirty thousand yards of cloth could be produced each day. The enormous weaving shed contained twelve hundred power looms at a time when a Bradford factory with six or seven hundred power looms was considered large.

The architects were Henry Lockwood and William Mawson, who had set up in partnership in Bradford only a year before Salt commissioned the first plans for his mill from them in 1850. They were to be responsible for the design of much of the village of Saltaire, and

for many notable public and industrial buildings in Bradford, including St George's Hall (1853), the Wool Exchange (1867), and the Town Hall (1873). Their other buildings show that Lockwood and Mawson were capable of designing in a variety of styles, including classical and gothic. For the mill at Saltaire, however, they chose a style they described as "Italianate", which drew many features from the renaissance buildings of northern Italy.

The mill is constructed in the warm local sandstone. Its architecture is strongly symmetrical, with lavish use of round-headed windows, corner pilasters, rustication, and, above the enormous, six story, south facade, two decorative lanterns with open sides and low-pitched, pyramid roofs. The two hundred and fifty foot chimney, placed a little apart from the main building, was originally topped with a magnificent decorated cornice. Even the cast-iron pillars that support the floors and roofs are decorated.

The detailing and ornament are restrained, but Salt's mill is a deliberate architectural creation, strikingly different from the unadorned factory buildings that were the norm in mid-nineteenth century Bradford. In this, as in so many other respects, Salt was an innovator. Bradford's more flamboyant mill buildings

The mill: south front.

were mostly erected later, like Samuel Cunliffe Lister's Manningham Mills of 1873.

Conveniently located for transport with the canal on one side and the railway on the other, the mill was designed according to the best engineering principles of the time. Careful attention was paid to efficiency, pollution and safety. William Fairburn, a famous Manchester civil and mechanical engineer who had designed cotton mills in Lancashire, advised on the layout and the internal structure of the mill. The internal construction was fire-proof, mainly using brick and cast iron. Special equipment was installed to reduce the output of smoke from the chimney. The drive shafts to many of the machines were deliberately placed under the floors, thereby reducing the danger of industrial accidents. Power was supplied from four steam engines placed in two elaborately decorated engine houses in the middle of the long south front. Originally the engines could be seen at work from passing railway trains through enormous arched windows made from expensive plate glass.

Work.

By the standards of the mid-nineteenth century the Saltaire works was a model factory, light

The mill: decorative lanterns.

and airy, well-heated and well-ventilated. What was it like to work there?

At peak employment, about 3,200 people worked in the mill. Detailed information about the workforce does not survive, but it is clear that during its nineteenth-century heyday a large majority of the workers were either children under the age of sixteen or young adult women. They predominated in the basic unskilled or semi-skilled production jobs of tending the spinning and weaving machines. They were the foot soldiers in Salt's industrial army and it was they, rather than the men, who marched to the relentless pace of the machines. Yet women and children did not dominate the workforce, despite forming a clear majority of it. Adult men filled the skilled jobs and the positions of authority. The managers, foremen and overlookers were overwhelmingly men, as were the wool sorters, mechanics, finishers, joiners and office staff. One consequence of this pattern of employment was a shortage of work for unskilled adult men, a social problem that was common to the worsted industry as a whole.

Skilled workers received higher wages than the unskilled, and men more than women. Overlookers, mechanics and some skilled workmen earned as much as 28 shillings per week.

Two fourteen year-old winders at Salts, 1930.

Workers leaving the mill in the early 1950s.

Warehousemen and male weavers, 14 to 16 shillings per week. Women were paid much less, spinners, weavers and combers receiving weekly wages of about nine shillings. Half-time children were paid two to four shillings per week. It is hard to convert these sums into modern money, because the denomination and the value of money have changed so much. Nevertheless, the contrasts in pay between the different grades of worker are clear enough.

Work at Salt's mill was arduous. In the 1860s it began at 6 am every weekday and finished twelve hours later at 6 pm, with two breaks amounting to an hour and a half for breakfast and lunch. On Saturdays work ended at 2 pm. Children started work in the mill at the age of eight, although until the age of thirteen only on a half-time basis. The other half of the working day they spent at school.

Long hours of work and part-time employment of children were not, of course, confined to Saltaire. In these respects the Saltaire mill was no different from other factories in the Bradford area. Salt's elevated conception of his responsibilities as an employer did not extend to offering terms of employment that were drastically superior to those of other factory masters in the Bradford industry. Rates of pay at Saltaire were broadly similar to those elsewhere in the district. Discipline in the mill was strict.

Despite its rigours, employment at Salt's held considerable attractions. There was little overt expression of discontent about pay or other issues from the workforce (although the fact that a majority of the workforce lived in Salt's company village may have inhibited the voicing of grievances against the firm). Only two strikes took place during the first thirty years of the mill's existence, and they were brief. The high death rate from anthrax among woolsorters brought about occasional agitation, but the lack of medical knowledge about the disease prevented any effective action. What is most noteworthy about the mill's early years is the quality and the loyalty of the workforce. Salt was able to demand very high standards of competence from his workpeople. New workers who failed to come up to standard during a trial period were dismissed. In the words of one power loom weaver, "they must be fearful good weavers to weave at Saltaire - they must be that." These carefully chosen workers demonstrated great loyalty to Salt. Many who came to Saltaire had previously worked for Salt in Bradford. Once at Saltaire, they tended to stay. By mid-nineteenth century standards, Salt's workforce was markedly stable.

If Salt paid wages no higher than those of other Bradford employers and worked his hands for the same long hours as they did, what was it that lured good workers to his mill and kept them there? The attractions of work at Salt's were several. One of the most important was Salt's ability to provide continuity of employment. Like other employers in the Bradford worsted industry in the 1850s and 1860s, Salt cut wages and put his workers on short time when trading conditions were bad. But, as in the 1840s, his extraordinarily successful, high-quality product range must have enabled Salt to provide work on a more regular basis than many other local employers. Regularity of employment assured his workers higher incomes over the years than those available to millhands elsewhere, who were more likely to be laid off. Workers at the mill also benefited from the facilities Salt provided for the welfare of his employees. These included the well-ventilated and well-heated work-rooms, a sickness insurance scheme towards which the firm contributed, a dining hall opposite the mill offices on Victoria Road, and annual works outings, which took the entire workforce on visits to the seaside at Scarborough, to the Art Treasures Exhibition at Manchester, and to Salt's own mansion at Crow Nest, south of Bradford. Another incentive to work at Salt's was, of course, the opportunity to set up home in the company village of Saltaire.

Houses.

The mill came first. Only in 1854, once the mill was at work, did Salt turn his attention to the construction of his model village. The mill was the economic motor that generated the wealth necessary to promote Salt's vision of the social and moral improvement of the working classes. Nevertheless, it was the village that most clearly embodied that vision. Building it was to take the best part of the next twenty years.

The idea that a good environment could nourish virtue was not a new one. The first half of the nineteenth century saw great interest in co-operative communities, like those associated with the early socialist Robert Owen. Often the plans for such communities emphasised the moralising effects of the character, the design and the physical layout of houses, streets and public buildings. Nor was the provision of accommodation by an employer for his workers a novelty of the 1850s. Factory masters and coalowners had been building houses on a large scale for their workers since the later eighteenth century. It

Houses in Ada Street.

Houses in George Street.

was, however, in the years from 1840 to 1880 that the practice of company housing and ideas drawn from the co-operative communities were combined in such a way that together they exercised a powerful influence on employers, social reformers and politicians alike. During these years, the moral regeneration of the working classes became inextricably linked in the minds of educated men with the quality of working class housing. Good houses, it was argued, produced good people. As Charles Kingsley, the author of the *Water Babies,* said in a lecture in 1859, "You may breed a pig in a sty, ladies and gentlemen, and make a learned pig ... but you cannot breed a man in a sty and make a learned man of him ... in any true sense of the word a man at all."

By building healthy, decent houses for workers, along with morally uplifting public facilities such as schools and parks, a mill owner could discharge what people at all levels in mid-Victorian society saw as his responsibilities as a good employer. Of course, in doing so, the mill owner imposed on his workers the kind of improvement that people of his standing considered appropriate. Workers were rarely consulted on whether they wanted to be improved in this way. Moreover, employers usually retained effective control of the facilities they provided, despite efforts to encourage self-

Houses in Albert Road.

Houses in Caroline Street.

reliance among workers by means of friendly societies and the like. Trades unions were not welcomed. Paternalist and literally patronising, these policies were a far cry from the anti-capitalist spirit which informed the co-operative communities promoted by the socialist followers of Robert Owen. Nevertheless, this brand of employer paternalism enjoyed the approval and gratitude of many working men, although such workers may often have regarded efforts of this sort by an employer as no more than their proper entitlement. Samuel Kydd, an old Chartist journalist, wrote in the radical *Reynolds Newspaper* in 1857 on the subject of Saltaire,

"it is true that Mr Salt may not have done more than his duty as regards the working man ... yet it is well to take note of improvement, and render honour to whom it is due."

Of all the industrial settlements built by manufacturers in the third quarter of the nineteenth century, Saltaire was the most ambitious and the most famous. It was large. Although the village never housed all the workers at Salt's mill, when completed in 1871 it supported a population of between four and five thousand in 824 houses. The houses were built on a greenfield site of 49 acres, deliberately separated from the mill by the railway line.

Most of them still survive. They gently rise in row after row up the north-facing slope of the Aire valley, the whole site then, as now, enjoying a wonderful view across the river to the woods and fields on the southern slopes of Baildon Moor. But a visitor needs only to take a short walk among the terraced houses to realize that the grand vista can often be glimpsed only around street corners and across rooftops. By modern standards the site is cramped, the houses packed close together at a high density. Some of the houses in the centre of the village, like those on Ada Street, are positively mean; they are small, they lack gardens, and they are bare of ornament.

Yet at a time when much of Bradford's working class housing was built round closed courtyards, sometimes on the back-to-back principle, with poor sanitation, inadequate drainage and unpaved, putrid streets, even the smallest Saltaire houses were a great improvement. The difference was clear enough to Samuel Kydd when he walked through the streets of Saltaire in 1857. He was impressed that they were "open, regular and well-built." Saltaire's streets were paved and drained from the start. They were open-ended, ensuring the light and ventilation which Victorians considered essential for health. There were hardly any back-to-backs. By the standards of the day,

George Street: detail.

sanitation was excellent, each house enjoying a yard at the back with an outdoor lavatory, which was regularly cleared. This was at a time when even new houses in Bradford often had to share lavatory facilities. Smoke pollution was much less of a problem than in Bradford. The village was separated by hills from the town's smoky factory chimneys. The furnaces that drove the boilers at the Saltaire mill were designed to minimize smoke output. Not surprisingly, the village was markedly healthier than Bradford's working-class districts.

The houses were all rented to tenants by Salt's company on a weekly basis. The level of the weekly rent varied according to the size of the house. Rents were no more than those in Bradford, and sometimes rather less. The bulk of the housing consisted of what were termed workmen's houses, let for the lowest rent and very basic in facilities. Workmen's houses, like those in Ada Street, had two stories, with a living room, kitchen and two (later sometimes three) bedrooms. More expensive houses, termed overlookers' houses, had a scullery, kitchen, living room, three bedrooms and a very small front garden. Good examples are in George Street and William Henry Street. The finest houses in the village were those that formed its western boundary along Albert Road, furthest from the mill and facing away

from it westwards towards open country. These had larger gardens, more rooms and were intended for the firm's executives, such as cloth managers, designers, and wool buyers.

Despite the terminology, the share-out of tenancies was not strictly ordered according to the hierarchy of employment within the factory. There were always more overlookers and skilled workmen than could be accommodated in "overlookers'" houses. Some of the lower paid workers managed to secure tenancies in the better class of houses. One key reason for such apparent discrepancies was the size of mid-Victorian families. Families with four or five children were common. Those children could earn from the age of eight. The rent a family could afford often depended not so much on the father's earnings, but on the number of earners in the family. Nevertheless, a family of seven must have been cramped, even if they managed to secure the tenancy of one of the better class of houses with three bedrooms and a scullery.

The proprietorial, paternal nature of the relationship envisaged by Titus Salt between himself and the tenants in his company village was emphasised in the names of its streets. Caroline Street, George Street, Ada Street, Constance Street: these and most of the rest were named after members of his family – his wife, his children and his grandchildren. Yet there were limits to his paternalism. In contrast to many a country squire and some paternalist millowners elsewhere in Yorkshire, Salt chose not to live close to his village. For most of his later life he made his home at Crow Nest near Lightcliffe, ten miles south of Bradford, although for a few years he lived at Methley Hall, fourteen miles east of the town. However, his son, Titus junior, who was actively involved in the management of the firm and took over its leadership on his father's death in 1876, did build a mansion (now demolished) in 1872 at Milner Field, a short distance across the valley from Saltaire.

We have no evidence that the architecture of the village had special political or religious significance for Salt, but it is possible that it did. Although some of the houses are extremely plain, many are decorated with round-headed windows and doors in the same Italianate style as the mill. In an age of bitter religious and political divisions, architectural style could take on wide-ranging implications. In nearby Halifax, architecture became a vehicle for the expression of the political and religious rivalry between the town's two great millowning families - the Tory, Anglican Akroyds and the Liberal, nonconformist Crossleys. In the 1850s

a new Town Hall was proposed for Halifax. Edward Akroyd submitted a design in the Gothic style, representing hierarchy, tradition and order. The Crossleys, by contrast, submitted an Italianate design which evoked the independent, enquiring spirit of the Italian city states of the Renaissance. It may not, therefore, have been simply an aesthetic preference that pursuaded Salt, himself a Radical-Liberal and a nonconformist, to favour the Italianate style for Saltaire.

Rational and improving amenities.

Immorality and improvement, sin and redemption; these issues obsessed the early Victorians. Men and women at all levels of society agonised over what seemed to be a rising tide of vice, depravity and irreligion, especially among the labouring classes. It is important to emphasise that hostility to gambling, drinking and sexual excess, to "folly and vice", was not confined to the wealthy. Moral reformers existed at almost every level of society, although it is impossible to know how many working people embraced their views. The motives behind the reformers' efforts to inculcate morality and improvement were varied, but in practice those efforts shared many common elements. Among the working classes, men with widely differing objectives sought to promote a similar improving diet of temperance, decency and self-improvement among their fellow working men. Some were evangelical Christians, others Chartist activists. For the evangelicals the aim was spiritual salvation in Heaven; for the Chartists secular salvation through the ballot box.

The moral reform activities of wealthy men like Titus Salt shared many features with the efforts of working class advocates of moral regeneration, but in two respects they were different. First, wealthy moral reformers were motivated, at least to some degree, by their economic self-interest as profit-making employers of labour. They were concerned to ensure the discipline of their own workforces and the political stability of the manufacturing towns in which they were heavily outnumbered by the poor. Second, their wealth gave them far greater power than their poorer counterparts to create the conditions in which they believed men and women would be good.

Improved housing was one means to this virtuous goal, but Titus Salt never intended his village to be simply a barracks for his respectable, industrial regiment. Like many other moral reformers of the period, much of his effort was concentrated on the meagre

The Congregational Church.

The portico of the Congregational Church: detail.

leisure time available to the working classes. Leisure was a problem for men like Salt, who were advocates of the gospel of work. They recognised that leisure was necessary and beneficial for working people, but it always threatened to degenerate into idleness or worse. Leisure provided the temptations of improvidence, drunkenness, fornication, and violence, or, equally threatening, Chartist and socialist politics. Many wealthy men came to believe, therefore, in the necessity of providing the working classes with "rational" and "improving" ways of spending their leisure time. Uplifting forms of leisure would counteract the appeal of leisure activities the wealthy regarded as degrading, debasing and

threatening. Titus Salt was one of the most prominent advocates of this doctrine, as the public amenities he provided on such a scale at Saltaire demonstrate.

Salt's crusade against vice and depravity was inextricably tied up with his firmly-held non-conformist religious beliefs. Early-nineteenth century Christianity taught its followers to battle against sin. Encouraging people to attend public worship and spreading the Christian faith were crucial weapons in that battle. Appropriately, the first of the public buildings Salt provided at Saltaire was a six hundred seat church, completed in 1859 at a cost of £16,000. This, a church of his own Congregational denomination, is the most ornate building in the whole village, with a semi-circular portico, Corinthian columns, and a tower crowned with a dome. Its location, directly opposite the entrance to the mill, was carefully chosen. Church and factory, God and mammon, faced each other at the focal point of the village. Together they constituted a realisation in Yorkshire stone of the twin forces that had created Salt's model community: his Congregational faith and his economic success. Only a small minority of Salt's workers shared his Congregational beliefs. Salt, however, was not a denominational bigot. Many of his workpeople were Wesleyan Methodists and Salt provided land on Saltaire Road for an eight hundred capacity Methodist chapel (now demolished), which was completed in 1868. The £5,400 for the building was raised mainly by public subscription. Saltaire, therefore, was a community with abundant facilities for Christian worship in the manner of two of the principal nonconformist denominations. By no means all of the village's inhabitants regularly attended worship, but congregations were large.

Religion was the cornerstone of the moral community Salt sought to construct at Saltaire. It was closely buttressed by education. Salt, in common with much polite opinion in the

The School: detail.

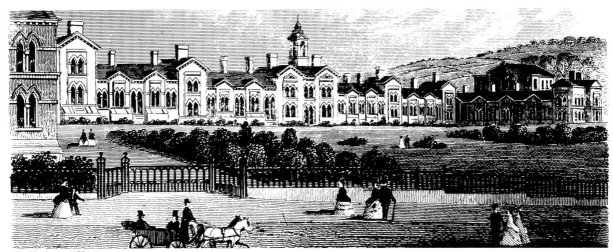

The Almshouses, 1874.

1840s, believed the moral and social evils overwhelming the new manufacturing towns were the result of ignorance among the great mass of the people. Consequently education was, to quote the *Bradford Observer,* a "sacred cause". Salt opened a school at Saltaire in 1854, which was housed in the dining hall (now Shipley College Annex). It was attended by children up to the age of thirteen, full-time by those less than eight years old and part-time by their older brothers and sisters who also worked in the mill. Under the Factory Acts, Salt was obliged to provide schooling for his younger workers, but it is clear that he was not one of those factory masters who begrudged making provision for education. In 1868 he

moved the school to new, purpose-built premises between Victoria Road and George Street, which housed approximately seven hundred pupils. The expensively decorated building has an elaborate frontage facing Victoria Road, with colonnades and a bell cote. Boys and girls were taught separately, the boys at one side and the girls at the other. In addition, Salt provided the site and £7,000 for a Congregational Sunday School (now demolished), built in 1875 at the corner of Caroline Street and Victoria Road with space for eight hundred children.

Victorian promoters of virtue, like Salt, were not concerned solely with the mental hygiene of the working classes. They believed that one of the most important reasons for moral depravity among working people was the dirt and disease which blighted their lives. Physical hygiene was therefore a major priority at Saltaire. In addition to providing well-serviced and well-ventilated housing, Salt built a bath and wash house (now demolished) on Amelia Street, at a cost of £7,000. It contained machines for washing clothes, drying facilities and twenty-four baths. Contrary to Salt's expectations, the facilities did not prove popular with the inhabitants of the village. They preferred to bath and wash at home, possibly for the sake of convenience, or perhaps to preserve the privacy which was so prized by respectable Victorians of all classes. The physical welfare of Salt's workers and the villagers was also provided for by a hospital, built in 1868 towards the top of Victoria Road.

Adjacent to the hospital are forty-five single story almshouses, opened in the same year, with their own chapel. They are built around a square to a profusely ornate design with gothic details, reflecting the Medieval origins of this kind of charitable institution. Up to sixty pensioners were accommodated here. They received a small weekly allowance from Salt and no rent was charged. To qualify for accommodation in the almshouses it was

The Almshouses: detail.

necessary to conform to Salt's standards of behaviour. Charity was provided only to those whom he considered genuinely to deserve it. Not only did the pensioners have to be incapable of work, but they had to display (and go on displaying) "good moral character".

Religion, education, charity; as the village grew during the 1850s and 1860s Salt supplied all three on an increasingly generous scale. But how did he deal with the villagers' leisure hours, the time when they might be tempted to succumb, like so many of their counterparts in Bradford, to sloth, inebriation, or lewd entertainment? Salt's solution was two-pronged. He refused to allow public houses in the village, but at the same time offered a range of alternative leisure facilities.

It is widely believed that Saltaire was a "dry" village and Salt a fanatical advocate of total abstinence from alcoholic drinks. Neither belief is true. Salt served wine in his own home and allowed an off-licence to trade in the village. He was a passionate advocate of temperance in the consumption of alcohol, but he did not try to enforce total abstinence. His main concern at Saltaire was to keep public houses and the rough culture associated with them out of the village. In common with many respectable Victorians, he regarded pubs as little more than

The Institute, 1874.

The Institute: detail.

schools of vice and poverty, places which positively encouraged working people to squander their livelihoods and to embrace every kind of depravity. Salt was also aware, however, that public houses were often the only places working men had available to meet socially, or to conduct the business of their communities.

As an alternative to the pub, Salt offered leisure facilities that were sober and improving, rational and respectable. Self-help was for Salt a virtue to be encouraged. He and his family supported a variety of clubs, including a horti-cultural society (allotments were available along the canal), a cricket club and a fishing club. But more important than any individual club was the Institute (now Victoria Hall) which he built opposite the school on Victoria Road between 1869 and 1871, at a cost of over £18,000. Its purpose was made clear in a prospectus provided for the villagers before its completion:

> "It is intended to supply the advantages
> of a public house without its evils; it
> will be a place to which you can resort
> for conversation, business, recreation
> and refreshment, as well as for
> education - elementary, technical and
> scientific. In the belief that 'it is gude to

The Institute: detail.

The Park, 1874.

be merrie and wise' provision is made for innocent and intelligent recreation."

The Institute is a large building, and was liberally decorated, inside and out. Patrons were enticed by a judicious mixture of sober entertainment and popular adult education, which was unique in nineteenth-century England. The Mechanics' Institutes established in many early Victorian towns were more exclusively (and severely) educational. Temperance pubs and public libraries offered a far narrower range of amenities. To educate, the Saltaire Institute provided a laboratory, a concert hall, a lecture theatre, a library with four thousand books, a school of art and classrooms. To entertain, it offered a reading room, chess and draughts rooms, smoking rooms, a billiards room, a bagatelle room and a gymnasium. Membership was cheap, two shillings a quarter for men and one shilling for women; so were the facilities, threepence a game being charged for billiards and the same sum for the rent of a room for an evening. The Institute enjoyed considerable success, becoming a focal point for the social life of the village. Three years after its opening it had over a thousand members and many clubs and societies used the building for their meetings.

The final component in Salt's plan for

disciplined, rational leisure was the park, opened in 1871 on a fourteen acre landscaped site across the river from the mill and the church. The park offered a wide range of recreational activities - swimming and boating on the river; bowls, archery, cricket and croquet on the open spaces - but this was to be orderly, respectable recreation. The fourteen acres were laid out in an ordered pattern of flower beds, walks, a terrace promenade and pavilions, with a large cricket pitch and areas for other sports. Rules were strict. On Sundays the park opened at 2 pm, to encourage people to attend church or chapel in the morning. Gambling, swearing, drunkenness and stone throwing were forbidden; so were dogs and unaccompanied children under eight.

Salt's vision of a sober, industrious "good life" permeated the whole of Saltaire. It found its most bountiful expression in the recreational amenities which offered an alternative to the world of the public house and the cheap dancing saloon. To provide that alternative, Salt was prepared to spend tens of thousands of pounds. This was in addition to the sum of over a hundred thousand pounds he spent on building the houses in the village. Why did he do it?

Why Saltaire?

It is rare for human beings to be entirely frank about their motives. It is especially difficult to re-construct the motivation of a man like Titus Salt, who was so reticent in public and has left us with so few of his private thoughts. Inevitably, therefore, controversy surrounds the question of why he built Saltaire. Should the village be interpreted simply as a piece of extraordinarily enlightened charity; was it, as Samuel Kydd the old Chartist claimed, no more than any decent employer should have done; or was it an act of studied largesse by a cynical capitalist, designed to secure a compliant, captive workforce?

A few things are clear. With the arrival of power woolcombing at the end of the 1840s, Salt had good reason to replace his scattered Bradford factories with a single, integrated plant. Moreover, he had sufficient wealth to do so. Saltaire offered an extremely advantageous location for manufacturing. Within a few yards of each other were the river Aire, to provide the water essential for many manufacturing processes, the Leeds-Liverpool canal, and the newly-opened railway. If the industrial potential of the site was to be exploited, some kind of new settlement had to be built to house the workers. At a pinch, it was possible for the mill to function with a workforce which travelled the three miles from Bradford. The mill operated in this way during the mid-1850s, immediately after it was opened and before much of Saltaire was built. But this was an era when most (though not all) workers were accustomed to live within a short walking distance of their place of employment. To run the huge new factory on a greenfield site so distant from Salt's existing plants in the heart of Bradford, housing had to be built, if not by Salt himself then by someone else.

Yet Saltaire was more than simply a barracks for Salt's industrial army. It was always an exercise in moral and social regeneration. Salt combined intense personal ambition with an overwhelming sense of duty. A profoundly religious man, he believed that his success as an entrepreneur was literally God-given. It was evidence that he was doing God's work, but God's work had to benefit others as well as himself. If amassing a great fortune was a sign of divine favour, it also imposed great obligations. By providing work and wages to his employees, Salt fulfilled some of these obligations, but he always felt more was demanded of him. He believed he should use the wealth and power God had given him to intervene in public affairs. Thereby he could help create the kind of environment in which others would lead virtuous, harmonious, and godly lives.

The problem for Salt at the end of the 1840s was how best to achieve this goal and where best to achieve it. Throughout that troubled decade he had been very active in the civic life of Bradford. He had held a number of prominent official positions, and in 1848 became the newly-incorporated town's second mayor. In terms of narrow party politics, he and his fellow nonconformist Radical-Liberals were extremely successful. Their efforts culminated in the incorporation of Bradford as a borough in 1847. In other ways, they failed the town. Environmental problems multiplied and Bradford was racked by the bitter and violent divisions associated with Chartism. Salt's personal campaigns on social and moral issues - reducing smoke pollution, providing a public park, investigating and improving the moral condition of the town - enjoyed only very limited success. At the end of the decade he confronted a moment of profound personal reassessment. Nearing the age of fifty, he was extremely wealthy. He contemplated retirement, but decided instead to move to Saltaire. It was not just business considerations that drew Salt there. At Saltaire he could pursue his reforming objectives on a scale he could manage himself, unhindered by the setbacks,

limitations and compromises that were inevitable in a large, growing town with problems as intractable as Bradford's.

This desire for personal authority and control is characteristic of Salt. He was a compassionate, philanthropic man, but compassion and philanthropy were to be dispensed on his terms. He genuinely desired the moral, intellectual and social improvement of working people, but held rigid views on how it should be achieved. He hoped to bring about the harmony between the classes which was missing in Bradford, but without relinquishing his own authority and that of men like him. Nevertheless, it would be wrong to dismiss his approach as entirely autocratic. Although he was guided by a sense of personal mission, a belief that he was doing God's work, his chosen role was that of a facilitator, helping working people to help themselves. He was a paternalist, not a tyrant.

Saltaire was more than Titus Salt, however. It cannot be understood simply by reconstructing his aims and his motives. The village consisted of its people. To understand nineteenth-century Saltaire, it is necessary to consider what Salt's paternalism meant for them. Unfortunately, we know surprisingly little about what individual villagers actually thought about the place. As with Salt himself, few of their private thoughts have been recorded. Consequently the question of what the village meant to its inhabitants has been subject to as much controversy as Salt's own motives.

What is certain is that there was very little overt opposition to Salt's regime at Saltaire. Strikes and other disputes were rare. Much more characteristic of life in the village were the extravagant displays of public gratitude offered by its inhabitants to Salt. At different times he was presented by the villagers with a bust, a portrait and addresses praising his conduct. The village turned out en masse for his funeral. He was generally acknowledged to be a good employer. It is, of course, possible that all this was a sham; that people were secretly resentful of Salt's overweening efforts to manage their lives, but were too frightened to express overt opposition. As both employer and landlord, Salt enjoyed enormous power over his workers. Employees dismissed from the mill could not go on living in the village. Yet what little evidence we have does not suggest a community living in fear, although it was a community that lived in a state of dependency. Saltaire people had a local reputation for being subservient to Salt. Fear of eviction may have played a part in generating deferential behaviour, but deference had a lot more to do with the considerable perks of life in the village and gratitude to Salt for providing them. After all, what Salt provided was better than virtually any other employer in the district. Not surprisingly, many of his employees identified with him, with his mill and with his village.

Was Saltaire, then, a "soft prison", where the political militancy of the Chartist years was bought off by good housing and other amenities? Was Salt's paternalism (consciously or not) ultimately a device for securing a compliant, captive workforce which could be indoctrinated into disciplined behaviour that ensured continued profits? These pejorative ways of characterising Saltaire may have an element of truth, but they are far from being the whole story. Salt did not have to move to Saltaire to secure disciplined workers. The firm would probably have prospered in the 1850s and 1860s even if amenities had not been provided there on such a lavish scale. Moreover, it is not clear that the disciplined, regulated tenor of life in Saltaire was something foisted on reluctant workers in order to shackle and constrain them. Rather it was something in which they colluded. Indeed, Salt was probably giving many of them what they wanted.

In spending to improve conditions for his workers, Salt was doing what the working-class radicals of the 1840s had criticised employers for failing to do. Indeed, he was doing what they often claimed employers would never do. He was acknowledging that the relationship between master and men amounted to more than simply the performance of a task for the payment of a wage. It is important to understand that workers in this period rarely judged their employers by the standards of the socialist egalitarianism that later was to find expression in the Labour Party. What they did expect from their employers was practical acknowledge-ment of mutual obligations above and beyond the wage contract. By later standards, those obligations may seem grossly unequal and Salt's benevolence merely the crumbs from a rich man's table. Nevertheless, every stone at Saltaire testified to Salt's acceptance of his obligations to his workpeople and their families. Few employers in mid-nineteenth century England fulfilled those responsibilities more generously.

The employee's responsibilities within this framework of mutual obligation were work, loyalty to the master and identification with his interests. It is no co-incidence that many of Salt's workers appear to have been noncon-formists like Salt himself. To think of Saltaire principally as a "soft prison" is to miss the point. Life at Saltaire was highly regulated.

That does not mean that Saltaire was a kind of super-efficient machine for manufacturing disciplined, productive workers. Nor does it mean that the villagers were reluctant converts to the regime of high Victorian respectability, persuaded to submit to it only by good housing and generous amenities. After all, any villagers who craved the pleasures which Saltaire denied them would have found it extremely easy to indulge. If they wanted to drink in a public house, there were many within a few minutes' walk. If they wanted to play dissolute games, the open fields beckoned over the wall of the park, and a short distance further on was Shipley Glen, a famous meeting place for Chartists and secularists.

For many of the village's inhabitants, the disciplined tenor of life at Saltaire was probably part of its appeal. It matched their own prejudices. Salt could afford to be very selective in his choice of employees. Workers who disliked the moralising aspects of life in the village were unlikely to apply for work there. It is probable, therefore, that those who worked for Salt often started out sympathising with many of his views. What Saltaire offered them was a segregated suburb, an island of respectability, where the dissolute were excluded. It is striking that very few of the poorest, most insecure and least respectable section of the working class, the casual labourers, lived there. In particular, there were hardly any Irish Catholic immigrants, who were universally associated with drunkenness and squalor. Saltaire is best characterised not as a device for imposing discipline on recalcitrant workers, but rather as a means of enhancing the morality of a select group of workers in a segregated setting.

Salt accrued a number of benefits from this state of affairs. It secured the continuing profitability of his business. It fulfilled the obligations he believed he owed his workers. It also provided him with a select moral laboratory. He used the results of his controlled experiment there to demonstrate to the world the validity of his ideas on social harmony and the improvement of the working classes. It was Saltaire that transformed Salt from a man with a local reputation as a philanthropic employer into an international celebrity.

Afterword.

Titus Salt died in 1876, aged 73. By this time Saltaire had been completed and plain Titus had become Sir Titus. He was internationally famous and immensely popular in Bradford. Over a hundred thousand people lined the route of his funeral cortege from his home at Crow Nest south of Bradford to Saltaire. He is buried in the small family mausoleum attached to the railway side of the Congregational church.

With Titus dead and the markets for worsteds changing fast, the Salt family's connection with Saltaire began to fall away. Only one of Salt's children, his youngest son Titus junior, demonstrated any aptitude for running the business or any interest in it. Already active in the firm before 1876, he took over from his father and ran it until his own death at the age of forty-five in 1887. His control of the firm coincided with the collapse of the market for the brilliant, lustrous fabrics on which his father had built the prosperity of the business. Women's fashion was turning to softer, draped dress materials. Saltaire began to produce the new fabrics and to diversify into other new lines, but change was difficult. The virtual closure of the American market in 1890, as a result of high tariffs, precipitated the firm's collapse. In 1892 it was put into liquidation, and the next year the mill and the village were bought by a consortium of Bradford businessmen.

By this time, the Salt family's connection with Saltaire had been almost completely severed.

The Mausoleum.

Titus Salt's older children had gradually moved away from the area. A succession of new owners ran the mill after 1893. The business was to prosper again during the early years of the twentieth century, the inter-war decades and the 1950s, but the distinctive paternalist ethos of Titus Salt's era, already under strain in the difficult years of the 1880s, was never fully revived. In the England of the twentieth century, the paternalism that created Saltaire no longer had the capacity to inspire the nation. Increasingly it was collective, state solutions to social problems that caught the public imagination, rather than Titus Salt and his spectacular demonstration of individual benevolence. During the economic crisis of the early 1930s, the houses in the village were sold off to raise capital for new machinery.

The decades after the Second World War were the great era of industrial consolidation in the textile industries. Small and medium-sized firms were gobbled up by larger enterprises. The Salts company followed this general trend, acquiring control of a number of lesser woollen textile companies in Yorkshire, Scotland and Ireland. By the late 1950s, the Saltaire mill was just one of a number of factories owned by the firm.

However, there were other, hungrier fish swimming in the same sea. In 1958 the Salts group was itself taken over by Illingworth, Morris and Company Ltd. Events were soon to prove that size guaranteed neither prosperity nor security. Bradford's textile industry went into a progressive decline from the mid-1960s. The response of the mill's new owners was to start reducing production at Saltaire. Twenty years later, textile manufacturing at the mill ceased altogether and the building was left empty

In the mid-1980s Titus Salt's mill faced a problem that was familiar throughout the north of England. What was to be done with an enormous, apparently old-fashioned industrial building when the economic task for which it was designed could no longer be sustained? Many nineteenth-century textile mills in Lancashire and Yorkshire have suffered demolition. Happily, the Saltaire factory escaped this fate. In 1987, most of the mill complex was acquired from Illingworth Morris by Salts Estates Ltd., a company owned by Jonathan Silver. Saltaire has since become a widely-admired example of how to re-use a historic industrial site in sympathetic and creative ways, without compromising its architectural integrity. A large part of the site is leased for industrial use;

where yarn was spun in the nineteenth century, electronic components are assembled at the end of the twentieth. A diner and a range of specialist shops have opened up other areas to the public. But it is the continuing policy of regeneration through the arts that has brought about the most spectacular transformations in the use of the mill. The 1853 Gallery provides a permanent display of the works of one of Bradford's most famous sons, the artist David Hockney. A second gallery has hosted exhibitions of his latest work. Opera North has mounted a community production of West Side Story in the mill and two of Tony Harrison's plays have been presented there: The Royal National Theatre's production of *The Trackers of Oxyrhynchus* and Salts Estates' production of *Poetry or Bust,* a play about the nineteenth-century local poet, John Nicholson, performed by Northern Broadsides.

Yet in putting the mill to dramatically new uses, the influence of Titus Salt remains apparent. Salt chose a site for his mill that was physically attractive and enjoyed good communications. The mill was expensively built to an extremely high standard. The workrooms were designed to be light and airy. The Saltaire factory continues to bene-fit from all these advantages nearly a century and a half later. Even as it undergoes a transformation, Titus Salt's mill still bears witness to the extraordinary vision and ambition of its creator.

David Hockney in 1853 Gallery Salts Mill, 1994.